The Teig ... ey

of yesteryear

Chips Barber

Have you ever been to Devon?
Where the Teign flows crystal clear
Over stones and under bridges,
Spraying droplets like a tear.
It rushes, cascades, twisting,
Ever going on and on,
Getting nowhere in particular,
There it is – and now it's gone.
It travels over moorland,
Past the heather and the tors,
Then on through little villages,
With roses round the doors.
If you have never been to Devon,
Through the Valley of the Teign,
Then you have missed a treasure,
'Tis the prettiest you have seen.

Mavis Piller

OBELISK PUBLICATIONS

ALSO BY THE AUTHOR

The Lost City of Exeter
Diary of a Dartmoor Walker / Diary of a Devonshire Walker
The Great Little Dartmoor Book / The Great Little Exeter Book
The Great Little Plymouth Book / The Great Little Totnes Book
The Great Little Chagford Book
Made in Devon *(with David FitzGerald)*
Torbay in Colour / Plymouth in Colour
Beautiful Dartmoor / Beautiful Exeter
Dark and Dastardly Dartmoor *(with Sally Barber)*
Weird and Wonderful Dartmoor *(with Sally Barber)*
Ghastly and Ghostly Devon *(with Sally Barber)*
The Ghosts of Exeter *(with Sally Barber)*
Ten Family Walks on Dartmoor *(with Sally Barber)*
Ten Family Walks in East Devon *(with Sally Barber)*
Burgh Island and Bigbury Bay *(with Judy Chard)*
Tales of the Teign *(with Judy Chard)*
Dawlish and Dawlish Warren / The South Hams
Torquay / Paignton / Brixham
Around & About Salcombe
Around & About Seaton and Beer
Around & About Sidmouth
Around & About Teignmouth and Shaldon
Topsham Past and Present
From the Dart to the Start
Dartmouth and Kingswear
Cranmere Pool – The First Dartmoor Letterbox

For further details of these or any of our titles, please send an SAE to Obelisk Publications at the address below, or telephone Exeter 468556.

All photos belong to Mavis Piller apart from pages 3, 4 (top), 7 (bottom), 8 (top + bottom right), 17 (bottom), 31 and 32 (bottom) which belong to Chips Barber. Page 11 (top) was provided by Gertrude Shove.

First published in 1994
by Obelisk Publications, 2 Church Hill, Pinhoe, Exeter, Devon
Designed by Chips and Sally Barber
Typeset by Sally Barber
Printed in Great Britain by
Maslands Ltd, Tiverton, Devon

The Teign Valley
of Yesteryear

The Teign Valley is one of the loveliest natural corridors in Devon, carving out a deep depression in the landscape for much of its course. The River Teign is about thirty miles in length and down through the centuries people have carried on a generally quiet existence in and around its valley.

This book is very simple and straightforward in its format, for it is a nostalgic trip from the upper reaches of the river, on the edge of the high moors, to the point where the Teign's waters mingle with the arm of the sea in the shape of the Teign Estuary. The book is packed with old postcard and photographic views from places along the river's course. Some places have changed greatly whilst others live on almost unaffected by the never-ending march of time. But you must judge for yourself if the places in 'The Teign Valley of Yesteryear', as shown by these marvellous old views, is the same place today. We hope that you will enjoy the journey from the heights of Dartmoor down to the lowlands at Newton Abbot. In between there is some grand scenery and wonderful villages.

GIDLEIGH CASTLE HOUSE, CHAGFORD

This first view is of the ruins of Gidleigh Castle. It was not very highly rated by the Ward Lock Guide for the 1930s as it had this to say of it: "The ruins of Gidleigh Castle are close by in a farmyard. The Castle could not have been a very important one, and the chief remains are a late thirteenth-century tower with a vaulted basement. A rather insecure staircase leads to an upper floor, where is a fireplace, with ash trees springing from the wall on each side." Now you know!

The Teign starts as two main flows, the South Teign that rises just above Fernworthy Reservoir, and the North Teign that has its beginnings high on one of the most elevated plateaux of the northern moors, less than a mile to the south-south-east of the legendary Cranmere Pool. The two rivers join together near Chagford, the place featured in these two pictures.

Chagford has been an inland resort and enjoyed a boom in Victorian times as the railways made travel a more pleasant and practicable experience. Although Chagford never was linked to the railway network, despite some grandiose schemes to do this, it was served by one of the earliest bus services to reach out to the moors. The view below is taken just up the road from The Square, beside the church wall, at a time when life passed by at a more leisurely pace.

The top view is taken from almost the same spot as the last one. However this one is looking towards The Square at Chagford and features The Three Crowns Hotel on the left hand side of the road. This famous old inn has its ghosts. If you ever visit it keep an eye out for Mary Whiddon, a poor girl shot dead on her wedding day at the nearby church, and also for unfortunate Sidney Godolphin, a Royalist shot dead in the porch of this hostelry during the civil war. Both were killed within a year or two of each other and both have been known to haunt the inn!

Below Chagford the Teign babbles its way past the farmyard (shown below) at Rushford Mill. Note the stepping stones that were far more prominent in the past, affording a dry passage across the river – except, that is, in times of flood.

Drewsteignton is a picturesque little hilltop village and lies on the winding, roller-coaster road from Chagford to Exeter. The above photograph is taken at a point where that road enters the village, close to where the village school was located. This is now a private residence. Although the street appears to be deserted, closer inspection will reveal that several villagers were curious to see a photograph being taken as this was something of a novelty at that time. A lady and her dog are on the left whilst another pair of young ladies are stood in their doorway.

Below is a slightly fading picture taken near the church gate. Both these views, and many others in the book, were the skilled works of the postcard firm of Chapman & Son of Dawlish who had an affinity with this part of Devon.

Despite having 'teign' as part of its name, Drewsteignton stands a tidy distance away from the river. If you walk from the village, either down the lane to Fingle Bridge or

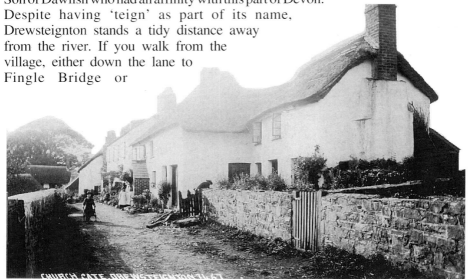

perhaps, more energetically, take part of the Two Moors Way into The Teign Gorge, you'll know what we mean. Above is the standard view that appears in most books whenever Drewsteignton is featured. The card actually states the pub's name as being the Druids Arms. The picture would have been taken when 'Aunt Mabel', legendary licensee for a great many decades, was just a girl.

Below is a view of the Teign Gorge taken from The Hunters' Path, near Castle Drogo, looking towards Sharp Tor. Today this is a much more wooded scene. The postcard's caption states that this is Fingle Glen but this should not be confused with the golf course and leisure complex, of the same name, that is at Tedburn St Mary today.

This is a view showing Sharp Tor in the foreground with a much narrower Hunters' Path going over its summit. Beyond and above it is the wooded spur where Castle Drogo has since been built. Below are two views of the tea shelter at Fingle Bridge, now the site of the Anglers' Rest.

PINGLE BRIDGE & GORGE OF THE TEIGN, DARTMOOR.

The next road bridge downstream is Clifford Bridge where a sign on the wall of the farm points thirsty travellers to refreshment in the form of 'Teas'. Originally cider was made here but today the principal activity is that of a camping and caravan park set in the loveliest of meadows beside the River Teign. The stream in the picture is but a small tributary and is shown just yards from where it joins the larger river.

CLIFFORD BRIDGE FARM, DREWSTEIGNTON.

The road from Exeter to Moretonhampstead crosses the River Teign at Steps Bridge. The above picture shows the original tea gardens where many charabanc crowds and pedal-weary cyclists enjoyed a refreshing wayside stop in idyllic surroundings. Below all the children have donned their Sunday best to extend a very special 'Welcome to Dunsford' to the Prince and Princess of Wales, returning from a visit to Dartmoor. Soon afterwards they became King George V and Queen Mary.

The Teign Valley

Dunsford, S. Devon.

Dunsford sits snugly in the lee of the higher moors and as a result has a much more tolerable climate. The village is where the River Teign gets tired of following its west-east course and begins to veer around to follow a more southerly route between the canyon-like hills that tower above it.

Dunsford's population, since 1801, has generally fluctuated between 500 and 700, its peak though being shown in the census of 1851 when it reached 977. The photo below shows the old post office. To the left of the tree is the current post office.

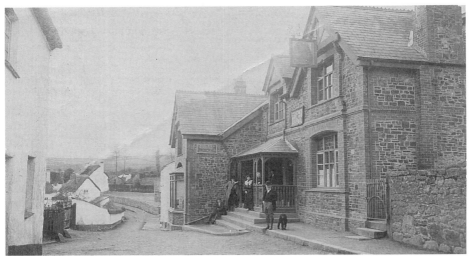

These two views of Dunsford were taken in an age when life was not ruled by the motor car. Then village life, as in all these Teign Valley villages, was far more self-contained with people working in the immediate area and not in distant towns like Newton Abbot and Exeter. These two pictures are the reverse of each other. The top view (1910) looks from the imposing Royal Oak, on the right, downhill on the road that leads out of the village towards Clifford Bridge, whilst the other one looks up the hill towards the village pub and church. An inspection of the outside of the pub, many years on since this was taken, will show that the entrance is now behind the man with the dog. The pub sign appears to have survived the years but has been moved to the far gable end of the pub. Just to the right of the inn is a wrought iron gate, above two steps, which leads up to the church. The steps have gone and the same gate has been re-hung just a yard or two back. The white cottages towards the back left are now partly obscured from the spot where this was taken, by a village hall that has since been built.

As the crow flies, Bridford is just over a mile from Dunsford but the journey between these near neighbours makes it seem a lot farther than that! Bridford is up in the hills and in the past had something of a reputation for being behind the times. It is believed that when a past King of England died, the news took six weeks to reach this village. Most of the people who lived there in the past were actively engaged in farming, or toiled in the granite quarries in the parish or worked in the barytes mines of the district. Their contact and knowledge of the 'outside world' was limited but that was then. Now a lot of Bridford's villagers commute to work in the bigger centres of population. Both these old views feature the church, which is dedicated to St Thomas Becket. As it is set in such beautiful countryside, it's not surprising to note that a lot of new homes have been built in and around the village.

Now it's a well known fact that neither Alphington nor Ide are in the Teign Valley. However, for a little more than half a century, these two villages were linked to the valley by a branch line, which ran from the main line, just outside St Thomas Station, through Marsh Barton, Alphington, Ide and then Longdown before heading on south-westwards to reach the Teign Valley proper. Throughout the rest of this little book the railway is a major feature in the collection of photographs. It was a lifeline to some, a regular form of transport for others and a route of great beauty for those who just wanted a pleasant, but slow, rail journey to Newton Abbot. Pictures of Alphington's tiny halt are rare and in this one the line is looking back towards the city with the gasometer, sited beside the Exeter Canal, visible in the distance. The picture below is taken from Constitution Hill and shows the view, before the A30 dual carriageway was built, across to Ide.

This is Ide's railway station, now a quiet cul-de-sac of attractive bungalows. The arrival of the railway line caused the nearest pub in the village to change its name from the New Inn to the Railway Inn. The station building at Ide was demolished in 1956, some two years before the closure of the line and Ide suffered

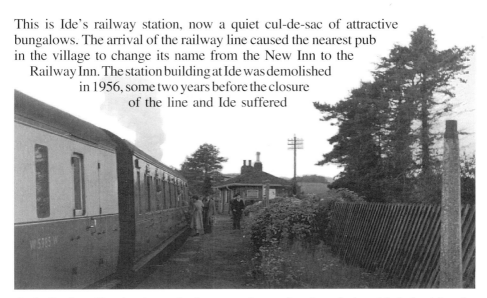

the indignity of having its station's status changed to that of a humble halt. After the railway's permanent departure, in 1958, the Railway Inn became the Poachers! The railway route was engineered to pass through the top of the village, bits of the route still being easy to identify despite the passing of many years since it was taken up. Several Ide villagers were employed on the railway – Bill Down, Alf Hallett, Sid Beer and Mark Bond to name but a handful of names from the railway's past. The route out to Longdown was regarded as one of the prettiest and certainly greenest of any lines in the area. The picture below shows the former post office at Dunchideock, which many people today like to stop and photograph. It's shown here with four legged, one horse-powered modes of transport as the norm. Is the cart on the way to the world-famous Dunchideock treacle mines located just along the road?

POST OFFICE, DUNCHIDEOCK.

The road from Exeter to the Teign Valley climbs steeply westwards from Pocombe Bridge, on the outskirts of the city, to follow a mile long ridge to the small village of Longdown, well known today for its wonderful village hall. The picture here shows the

village pub – the Lamb Inn. Although the appearance of the building is still very similar, there have been small, subtle changes like the addition of shutters. On the far right are shown some cottages that are no longer there, having been replaced by newer houses. The village, like many that were served by the railway, was well away from its station, shown here also. The setting for the station was unusual as the railway engineers were obliged to excavate one long tunnel, Culver, and one even longer one, Perridge, for the trains to pass through the narrow neck of high land between the watersheds that fed the Exe and Teign. Longdown Station was sited between the two tunnels in a sheltered location, but about half a mile from the village. During the interwar period, fresh flowers were often on sale on the platform.

This superb tower commands one of the best views in Devon; from its lofty summit it peers down on the Teign Valley way below. Although its correct name is Lawrence Castle (named after General Stringer Lawrence who founded the British Empire in India), many people refer to it as The Belvedere. The tower was built as a memorial to him as this was a favourite spot that he liked to visit when exercising his dog. Although he was not a resident of Devon, he came to the county many times to visit his friend, Robert Palk, at Haldon House on the Exeter side of the hill.

For many years the tower was occupied by two brothers called Dale. There was a third brother who lived in nearby Ide but a family rift meant that despite living almost within sight of each other, there was no communication between them.

It was built in the eighteenth century but rather than give away too many of its secrets here, we recommend that you pay your own visit; it's well worth it for the view from the top, once you have scaled the spiral staircase. Hopefully, Lawrence Castle will remain open to the public in the future. A distinctive landmark, it can be seen from many distant locations such as Exmoor, Dartmoor, East Devon and even from some of the higher hills in Somerset.

The hill on which it stands is Pen Hill and Marconi experimented from here when staying at Haldon House.

The railway had to avoid the dizzy heights of the Haldon escarpment so the railway builders used natural depressions where possible. Above is Dunsford Halt, opened 16 January 1928 and is shown to be as basic a stopping place as could be imagined. Passengers alighting here for Dunsford would have had an energetic march of almost two miles to the village. If they hadn't realised, before now, that Devon was a hilly county, then this exercise would have helped to register the fact! Had some people achieved their goal, this would never have been the situation for there were plans, long ago, to take the railway from this point to Dunsford and along the Teign Gorge up to Chagford.

On the bottom, opposite, is a lofty view of Christow, almost an alpine village in Devonshire terms. In the past many of the villagers were actively engaged in mining as silver, lead, manganese and copper are all present deep within these hills. Unlike many villages, Christow sprawls over the hillsides with little rhyme or reason to its layout. With its lovely cottages and variety of styles of architecture, this makes it a place well worth exploring on foot. The reservoirs of Tottiford, Trenchford and Kennick, high on the plateau above Christow, have often been referred to as Devon's 'Little Switzerland' but that was probably a whim of somebody with a lively imagination!

The red brick Christow Station (below) is now a private residence and the line, between the two platforms, has been landscaped. It was a colourful place on 26 June 1903 when the first train out from Exeter carried many local dignitaries. It left Exeter at 3.40 pm; after various civic addresses it reached Christow. There were sports races held in the nearby fields accompanied by various bands, including the spick and span Christow Band. And when everyone had worked up an appetite and thirst there was a celebration tea for 500 guests. During the 1930s, special trains were sometimes run up the valley from Newton Abbot or out from Exeter to bring hundreds of people out to the Teign Valley to see or pick the wild daffodils that carpeted the meadows near the station.

Country stations that today would not have any resident staff, once boasted quite a personnel. Here are the 'lads' from Christow Station. The message that accompanied the original card, from which this photo was taken, simply says this, and nothing else, and isn't even signed: "Dear M, How are 'ee? What do you think of G A H and his staff? What oh!" In the station's busiest days there was much activity with cattle being held in pens there waiting to go to market and an aerial ropeway coming down from the hilltop quarries above to bring down basalt ready to transport away by rail. When the last train ran, local schoolchildren showed their disgust at the line's passing by walking up and down the platform wearing sandwich boards as a form of visible protest.

Despite its lack of size Ashton is divided into two parts, about half a mile apart, Higher and Lower Ashton. The top picture is of Higher Ashton and shows the parish church of St John the Baptist. Although this view doesn't show it, because it's from the other side, this church is perched on a high spur of land and is an impressive feature when seen from its west side. The late, great professor and local historian, W. G. Hoskins, a man who always knew what he was talking about, referred to it as one of the most "atmospheric" village churches in Devon. The bottom view of the post office at Ashton and was one that took the fancy of "Nellie", who was staying at Clampitt House at Bridford. She sent it to her friend at Weymouth on 29 July 1913 during a spell of hot dry weather. This we know because she complained of the intense heat. Ashton was a picture postcard manufacturers' dream with its attractive whitewashed, thatched cottages.

The station at Ashton was, originally, the railway terminus for this line and passengers travelling up from the Newton Abbot direction could go no farther. The line was first opened in 1882 but only became a through route some twenty-two years later in 1904, this being late in terms of the spread of the railway network. The station could claim the unique distinction of being the only one on this branch line to have its own engine shed! In early 1958, as the threat of closure loomed over this line, the station was freshly painted in April to make it look smart – two months later it closed!

There are many who mourn the passing of branch lines like this one. It would have made a great tourist attraction, or it would have been useful when the main coastal line was out of action through storm, tempest, flood or landslip. It may even have been adapted to the modern phenomenon of park and ride. Those who live in the Teign valley villages know all about the problems of crawling into Exeter or Newton Abbot at peak times. The picture below shows the train leaving Ashton's station.

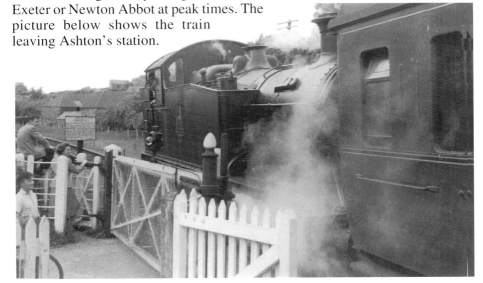

Here we have two views of the picturesque village of Trusham, snugly situated in the narrow valley of a small stream called the Tame that trickles south westwards to join the Teign. It's a small village, which just managed to top the 200 population figure in 1851. The top and bottom views appeared on cards posted at Trusham in November 1912 to someone in the Isolation Hospital in distant Newton Abbot.

In the bottom picture it's just possible to identify the church tower protruding heavenwards just right of centre. This small place of worship is dedicated to St Michael. Although not shown in either of these views, Trusham's war memorial, at the bottom of the village, is unusual in respect that the twenty-five men who came home from the war used their combined skills to erect it. Some quarried the stone, others assembled it, whilst some were involved in inscribing it to the memory of their fallen friends and relations.

Trusham was regarded as the most important station on this branch line with its fine signal box, which can be seen here. A clue to its importance appears in the photograph above – the quarries of the district were productive with a lot of minerals and stone being transported from here by rail. The Teign Valley Granite Company were the biggest company to transport their products on this railway. Four special trains were laid on daily to convey the materials. About 150 wagons could be accommodated in the sidings at Trusham. Micaceous haematite (high grade iron ore) was extracted at Great Rock Mine and the ores were also transported from Trusham. Scatter Rock Quarry was high up in the hills and their wagons were also seen trundling along the line with these words written on them: "Proprietors of the toughest stone on record". Silver, lead and manganese has also been extracted from this valley.

These two fine buildings are close to each other. Above is Canonteign Barton, or Old Canonteign. Its name originates from the canons of St Mary du Val in Normandy who were the fortunate recipients of this Domesday manor. Later the estate was owned by the Black Canons of Merton. During the English Civil War it was turned into something resembling a fortress by the King's men but was still taken by Fairfax. The house was built of local stone and served Sir Edward Pellew, the first Viscount Exmouth, until 1812. However the house was showing signs of decay so drastic action was necessary. He decided to build a new Canonteign House, pictured below, just a stone's throw away. Consequently Old Canonteign lost its aristocratic feel when it afterwards became a farm.

The newer Canonteign, with a distinctive Grecian appearance, is an impressive edifice as the picture shows.

Hennock.

Hennock stands high on the western shoulder of the Teign Valley with many of its houses enjoying tremendous views eastwards to the Haldon Hills or southwards over the Bovey Basin. Hennock's church (St Mary) once had a vicar, John Hill, who held the living there for fifty years. He had two sons, both of whom were involved in major war conflicts , including the battles of Waterloo and Trafalgar. Both came through unscathed and both lived to be over a hundred years old! The bottom photograph shows the little-changed Teign Village, less than half a mile below Hennock, with its one street of industrial-looking houses being something of a surprise settlement in so rural an area.

TEIGN VILLAGE

Having visited several smaller villages on our way down the valley since leaving Chagford, we now reach the relative metropolis of Chudleigh, which probably owes its larger size, today, to its closeness to the A38 road from Exeter to Plymouth.

The two views on this page are similar. The upper one is more recent with its better surfaced road, additional street furniture, and slightly more modern style of dress. It's also taken closer to the middle of the day for the shadows are shorter. The bottom, older card was posted on 14 August 1928 to someone in Tasmania so has been half way around the world before coming home. The Clifford Arms, on the right, is now The Coaching House.

This was taken in the days before Chudleigh had a bypass to ease its traffic problems. The parish church lies to the right of the top centre. The car park in the centre of the town is nonexistent in this view and around the town other places, which were spaces then, are now developed, particularly in that area of the top centre of the photograph. The two roads forking off towards the bottom left are the old, and less-old, road towards Exeter.

Chudleigh has always been a keen place for its sports but here the spectators seem more interested in the photographer than this 1912 cricket match!

"View from Rocks, Chudleigh."

At Chudleigh there is a large outcrop of limestone that has served many uses in the past. It has been quarried for building purposes, and used as lime to sweeten the soils of the district. The steep rock faces have been a playground for those who like a challenge to climb them. And as limestone is a soluble rock, great caverns have been formed underground so that spelaeologists can explore the underground world.

Chudleigh Rocks.

The caption says 'Ugbrooke Park' when really it should strictly say Ugbrooke House for this view shows nothing of the wonderful surroundings of the Capability Brown-designed park and its fine lake. The house, about three quarters of a mile to the south-south-east of Chudleigh, has had a colourful and long past with people from a wide range of backgrounds having cause to be here for a variety of reasons. Agatha Christie first set eyes on the man who was to be her first husband at a party here. During the Second World War it was home to an evacuated school from the East End of London. After the war had ended, Ugbrooke, eventually, in 1952, became a hostel that accommodated disabled Polish soldiers of General Ander's army.

Chudleigh Station was not only in the Teign Valley but after periods of prolonged heavy rain was sometimes almost in the Teign itself! To counter this farther along from the station was a wooden platform reached by a raised gangway from a nearby lane, which was used when great pools of water lay outside on the approach to the station. The station is now little more than a memory as the A38 is built over the track bed of the railway and the station long since gone.

Above is the next scheduled stop along the line – Chudleigh Knighton Halt, opened 9 June 1928, with its very distinct pagoda-shaped roofed shed. Apparently, in its heyday, this was a well-used halt with several carriage loads of people regularly getting on or off the trains. The last passenger train ran on 7 June 1958, just two days short of exactly thirty years since the day the halt was opened.

The Teign Valley Railway had about another mile (or five minutes journey time) for most trains to run before reaching its junction with the Newton

Abbot–Moretonhampstead line at Heathfield Station, shown opposite. Heathfield has developed into a large trading estate that covers a lot of the heath land found in this part of the Bovey Basin. Although the railways initially gave some of the earlier industries some impetus, the presence of the A38 remains the most important factor these days. So here we are at the end of the Teign Valley line, some seventeen miles down the track from Exeter. Our friend the River Teign, the real natural link in this book, has hardly got a look in with the photographers of the past preoccupied with the villages and the railways along the route. Apart from the beauty spots in the higher reaches, there are not that many cards with river views available. Yet all the while the river has passed through quiet green meadows weaving past the numerous mines and quarries and ducking under the railway line on five occasions on its never-ending quest to reach its estuary at Newton.

DARTMOOR FROM NEWTON ABBOT.

Newton Abbot's town centre is on the flat but all around rise steep hills that yield splendid views of the surrounding countryside. This is just one of those views that looks towards Dartmoor. The twin peaks of Haytor are just discernible to the left of centre on the horizon. But it's the foreground that has changed so much. The large complex to the left is Bradley Mill with the rear of Mackrell's Almshouses standing in front of it. Since the photograph was taken, Newton has grown and spread considerably so that what appeared as the green and pleasant countryside of yesteryear is now built upon.

Newton Abbot sits on the southern edge of the Bovey Basin and most things seem to head towards it, or at least used to in the past – the railways, the roads, the rivers and even the sheep and cattle from off the hills and moors eventually got to Newton. And this book is no exception for this is where the Teign reaches its estuary and where the branch lines that have trundled down

their valleys between immense hills, finally arrive at this cosy, bustling market town. The picture above shows the damage inflicted on the station during the war. The photo below shows the branch line curving in from the bottom left to avoid the long since demolished power station. Newton Abbot's Station, towards the top right, has witnessed many farewells and it's appropriate that it's here we take our leave. Hopefully you enjoyed the journey down memory lane and along the lovely valley of the Teign.